857 Habits of Highly Irritating People

...And some cool ways to make them squirm

Ben Goode

Published by:
Apricot Press
Box 98
Nephi, Utah
84648

books@apricotpress.com
www.apricotpress.com

ISBN 1-885027-46-7

Illustrated & Designed by David Mecham
Printed in the United States of America

Forward

One of life's most useful skills is the ability to irritate the people who annoy you. For years I have studied the idiots who bug me. Here is your opportunity to learn from these people: the pros. As easy as it appears to be to annoy other people, it's not as simple as you might think. In fact, I have catalogued over 857 separate skills irritating people possess, most of which they have tried on me. I will write about many of them. I would like to write about the rest of them, but I don't know enough about them to fool anybody. So while advertising a book with 857 habits is not factually correct, instead of considering our oversight fraud or misrepresentation, we hope you will choose to think of it as harmless hyperbole like we do. And we hope it will persuade you to buy this book so we can continue to run our mediocre publishing business in this lousy economy.

An Effort At Full Disclosure

I think it's probably time here for some full disclosure: The truth is, I don't actually know how many irritating habits there really are in the world. In fact, I'm not exactly sure how many there are in this book. But, however many there may be, you can be sure, as always, that these habits

I've written about in this book are very entertaining habits and that you will get your money's worth. So just quit belly aching about my writing, (which is habit # 288.) If you don't like this book, instead of writing a nasty letter to me, or complaining to everybody you know, thereby hurting book sales, instead, when life gives you lemons, why not turn them into a sow's ear or something else useful to get your money's worth. Here is one more way of doing just that: Choose somebody you REALLY don't like. Spend the next week or two bragging up what an awesome book this is-and insist that everyone should read it. Then give it to him or her as a gift. Then, you can take great satisfaction in knowing how disappointed he or she will be when she reads it. This way at least you can have a good laugh at his expense.

Now that you mention it, this illustrates one of the practical uses of amazing value contained within this book: the capacity to use it to irritate the people who annoy you. You can be sure that we will promote this application ad-nauseum. Obviously, if you buy a book for someone and it turns out that it disappoints or offends him or her, this could technically counts as one of the "what you can do about it" sections written about in this book-assuming that the said person is one who irritates you. If you can't think of any *other use for this book, you should buy it for this reason alone. You can use this book literally, to irritate the people who irritate you. We are grinning ear to ear right now thinking about this potentially great concept. (Why we constantly refer to ourselves as "we" when there is really only one person sitting here plinking away on the computer is a mystery we are trying to figure out. We certainly do not want to give short shrift to and offend the voices in our head, for one thing, and if we should accidentally write something that gets someone upset, it's nice to know that we can pass the buck. At least we think that would work if we continually refer to ourselves in the plural. It has absolutely no chance as a strategy if we regularly refer to ourselves in the singular. We will continue to try and figure this one out.)*

One other warning is probably in order here. Before you go out and try many of these skills illustrated in this book, you should probably practice a little. And then you should probably pass them by somebody whose judgment is better than yours. I'm sure there are many such people out there in your world. This may keep you out of jail.

I should probably also mention that when I am irritated by someone and then get all worked up like this, it causes my blood pressure to go up, which, in turn causes my doctor and wife to launch a "Let's get Ben on a diet and exercise" campaign. And things often just escalate from there-including my blood pressure. Actually, I don't know why this should have any relevance to you, but if irritating people cause your blood pressure to rise, at least you know that you have someone with whom you can commiserate. I hope that makes you feel better. If it does, this will give you another reason to buy this book, and it will give us another reason to hype it. Enjoy!

- Ben Goode

Ben Goode

 **Putting the kitchen cabinet 2-inches below the top of your head so that every time you walk past that place you crack your noggin.**

What you can do to irritate this person: This is one of life's great, cruel ironies: One of the people who has caused you the greatest amount of pain, suffering and irritation in your life, may never even be knowable to you. It is entirely possible that since he finished work on your house he has changed careers, been incarcerated, or even deported. If you assume that he has been deported or incarcerated, you may be more at peace since you know that some form of justice will have been served. Besides that, whenever you crack your noggin on his handiwork, you can always choose the option of throwing a fit and being ornery and grumpy for days and weeks afterward, thereby deriving at least some satisfaction by punishing him vicariously through making life miserable for all of the innocent

1

people in your world. Whatever you do, don't linger in thought about the possibility that this person may still be at large, possibly even continuing to hang cabinets two inches below the top of many other innocent people's heads. Do not consider the fact that he may even hang the cabinets in your next house.

Moral Justification: They will all grow to become better, more understanding and patient people as they develop the skills to deal with the likes of you.

HABIT No.
2

Putting some object like a table leg, pair of boots, corner of a wall, or 100 pound sack of nails on the floor in the exact place where your toe will go when you are shuffling to the bathroom in the middle of the night.

There is no hell or punishment severe enough for this person, unless, of course this person happens to be you, in which case you can take comfort in the fact that he or she has been adequately punished by the pain and suffering from stubbing your toe on the object you left in the middle of the floor.

The habit of calling you late for meals.

The solution to this is outside the scope of this work. We are, however, working hard to expand our scope, thus hoping to someday get it into our sights. When we do, we hope that you will be among the first to find out.

Making you come to work to get paid.

"What you can do to irritate the person who makes you do this?" you ask: Obviously, there are many things, but one of the easiest, which will come naturally for many of my readers, is to do crappy work. That will teach him, unless of course you already do crappy work, in which case you better come up with something else to do to punish your boss, since this obviously doesn't bother him or he would have fired you already.

Moral justification: By doing crappy work you will save energy. You can use this extra reserve of energy to do other philanthropic things when you get off work such as being difficult and obnoxious, thereby helping the people you love develop better skills to be used in dealing with other difficult and obnoxious people. (See above.)

Returning your check just because you don't happen to have enough money in your account today to cover it.

Many of us absolutely hate it when some lame bank employee does this do us.

What you can do to irritate the person who does this: Since the actual person who returns your check probably works at the bank, you will want to try some banking humor to annoy him or her. One way of doing this is to not pay your car payment for a few months. In the event that you already don't pay your car payment, this will probably not generate much humor, and so you will have to come up with something else. You could try something like a bomb scare or wearing a nylon stocking over your head and by using a fake gun making everyone lie down in the safe and locking them, in or something. If you choose to do this, be sure and leave them in the vault with some cupcakes, a pizza, or some other cool snack so they don't get too mad at you, press charges, and send you to prison for 15 years...unless, of course, it is your goal in life to go to prison for fifteen years, in which case you can save yourself a lot of trouble by just continuing to write bad checks.

HABIT No. 6

The habit of beating the teams I am cheering for.

This is a big problem for me in my life at this time. If I knew what to do, you can be sure I would do it. They are pathetic.

HABIT No. 7

Whining... also known as "Grousing"

Today, like every other day in your life, you will probably ask someone, "How are you doing?"

You may or may not sincerely want to KNOW the truth about how she or he may actually be doing, but out of politeness, or habit, you did ask the question, thereby opening yourself up to some kind of answer. A common answer I get all the time is, "Can't complain."

To which I often reply, "Sure you can. I've heard you do it before."

To which he or she would often retort, "Yeah, but it won't do ay good."

As you can plainly see, this is a bunch of nonsense. The truth is, complaining does help. If it didn't many people would stop. And as you also know, most people won't stop complaining. In fact, normally this person to whom you wished a cheery greeting will most likely go ahead now and begin whining about something else. This is very irritating. And it's likely to continue forever because it pays so well.

Let's take for example, the weather, which is one of the favorite grousing topics. Many people grouse about the weather. I think we should give everybody a voting machine and let them vote for the exact kind of weather they want. In fact, technology may soon get to the point that we can control the weather. All the people screaming about global warming want us all to change the way we live to alter the weather, so even though some of these people aren't the sharpest tools in the sheds, they must believe it's possible. Anyway, since it is possible that some day someone may be able to control the weather, who it is that gets to control it is very important. The only fair way to decide who gets to control the weather is democratically, I believe.

If you think representative government is contentious and messy now, just wait until they are making decisions about the weather. Of course there are some that complain if the sun shines because they think it's too hot. At the same time there would be those who would be whining it's not hot enough. If all we ever get is sunshine, pretty soon everything will be burning up with the heat. Somewhere there is someone praying for rain.

If we were to do this weather thing democratically, if 51% want snow in July, they will get it. If 51% want perpetual sunshine, we'll get it, no matter if we're starving to death. If the news people on talk radio whip up a grass-roots movement and split off a sizeable faction that doesn't want rain or sun, but likes wind, no one will be able to put together a majority and we will wind up with weather gridlock and everyone will be unhappy. And of course, there will be whiny victims who will complain no matter what, which is what this habit is all about. The important thing is there are some things you can do to annoy the whiners in your life, which should make you feel better.

What you can do to irritate the whiners in your life: Whenever you have a conversation with them, whether whiney or not, hum or whistle the refrain from some really bad annoying song throughout the conversation. This will get it stuck in their heads. Then you can visit them at the asylum. Thereafter, every time you see this person, hum or whistle this obnoxious song. This will bring the madness back into his life for a few more days. In fact, after a while, every time this person sees you or even thinks of you, he or she will also think of this song, thereby getting this awful song stuck again in his or her head, or possibly even encouraging him to avoid you—a super cool win-win situation.

| HABIT No. 8 | **Your spouse, parents, or friends telling you what to do.** |

When people you know tell you what to do it puts you in an awkward position. It takes the option of actually doing the thing they tell you to do off the table for you. Sometimes that's fine, because their advice was stupid, but very often what they are telling you to do makes great sense. You may have even eventually got around to thinking of this option yourself. It may even be a great solution to a horrific dilemma in your life, and now you have to go out and do some stupid thing that you didn't want to in the first place, because they messed up and told you to do it.

On the other hand, sometimes everybody can see the right thing for you to do. It's obvious, but it was absolutely NOT what you wanted to do. In this case it turns out being told what to do is a good thing. They have told you to do it, so now you can do the stupid thing you wanted to do in the first place. These people who made the recommendation will then be the ones responsible, in case things go badly.

How to irritate this person: Do what they tell you to do, thank them for the advice, tell them that you are only doing this because they suggested it and that you respect them so much that you will follow their advice blindly, that you don't think it sounds like a very good idea, but because they recommended it, you are going to do it because it absolves you of any responsibility for the result. Then go out and do a ridiculously schlocky job of whatever it is that they told you to do, so that it doesn't work out at all. They will be completely responsible.

Actually, now that I think about it, this is a lot like the game of football when the offense gets the defense to jump off-sides and then snaps the ball. They know the play will be called back if they throw an interception or something, but if they connect on a long play, they can nullify the penalty and take the big play. They get to run a risky play with no risk at all on their part.

<table>
<tr><td>HABIT No.
20</td><td>**Being the perky cashier who takes your $1100.00 for repairing the u-joints on your pickup truck and then says, "Have a nice day!"**</td></tr>
</table>

What you can do about it: Since sarcasm begets sarcasm, a healthy dose of sarcasm will annoy her and make you feel better. Saying something to her like: "Bet you're proud of that zit on your nose." Or "The late renaissance fashion of chunky women must be coming back into style around here," would be a couple of examples.

Moral justification: You really do want to have a nice day, and sometimes nothing gets the day off on the right foot, after something like an $1100.00 repair bill of course, than a well placed tidbit of sarcasm. In medical circles it is sometimes known as "therapeutic sarcastic thought vocalization." As a note of warning, however justified you may be, caution is advised when in truck stops and foreign airports.

HABIT No. 21
Being faster than you at driving into the parking stall you had spotted before you can get there.

You have all had the experience of waiting fifteen minutes for some lady to buckle her eight kids into their car seats and then arranging her groceries in the back of the van in alphabetical order, then talking for a few minutes on her cell phone while you are waiting for her parking spot. Then, just as she's pulling out, some clown, who has just arrived and who hasn't waited for even two seconds spots the spot and zips into it from the opposite direction.

What you can do about it: I believe Hell has special punishments for the people who do this. You can just do nothing and wait for Hell to punish them…or you can take matters into your own hands and follow her home so you can turn a fifty-gallon-drum of cockroaches loose in her bedroom, or stuff a gerbil into the tailpipe of her car.

HABIT No. 22
Looking at me

There are times when this does not bother me, such as when everything is OK. At the times when my fly is open, when my clothes don't match, or when I have just said something really stupid, it is not OK. Unfortunately, there are many people who are not very bright and who cannot tell the difference between times when looking at me will bother me or not, or who do not care. So I am recommending that, just to be on the safe side, you should probably stop looking at me.

HABIT No. **23**	**Calling you way too early in the morning and asking, "Did I wake you up?"**

Which of course he did, but naturally, for some very odd reason you have not collected your mental faculties yet, and so you feel awkward admitting that you were actually sleeping, even if it's 4:30 A.M., and so you are compelled to lie and say, "no, no, I have been up for hours cleaning my fish tank and digging the foundation for my new workout gym. Of course they will never buy it because you sound just exactly like someone who just woke up, or like someone who is doing his Wolfman Jack or Jill imitation.

What you can do about it: This requires that you get even, and since he woke you up ridiculously early, fire should be fought with fire, and so the easy way to annoy this person is to call him at 2:30 A.M. ten or fifteen Sunday mornings in a row, and ask him if you just woke him up, all the while trying not to laugh.

Better yet, pay someone he doesn't know do it for you and to apologize for having the wrong number.

Calling in the morning to ask if they woke you up when you were indeed already up.

The problem here is nobody will believe you, even if you have been up for two hours, if you have not used your voice yet.

What you can do: Obviously, the secret here is making certain that your vocal chords are all warmed up no matter what time of the morning you get up. That way, when you get a call at a ridiculous hour of the morning, you will always SOUND as though you have been awake for a while. If you do this, you can always lie about how long you have been up if you want to.

How to warm up your vocal chords at ridiculous hours of the morning: The best way is to make it a habit to practice your auctioneering, hog calling, or yodeling first thing when you wake up, no matter how early that is. Never mind that you will wake up everybody else in the neighborhood, because undoubtedly they are dealing with this same problem and will naturally want to be awakened as early as possible to begin warming up their vocal chords, too, and in this way avoid the embarrassment of someone who calls them believing he or she just woke them up.

| HABIT No. **25** | # Writing me a ticket when I get caught speeding |

This is one of the top 10 most irritating things in my life. And don't give me that line about he's only doing his job, because there have been occasions when I have been pulled over for speeding and the officer has chosen not to write me a ticket. So I know that writing the ticket isn't mandatory. Anyway, you all know how annoying this can be, so here's what we can do about it. Obviously, if gas prices continue to go up like they have the past few years, pretty soon no one will be able to afford to drive anyway, and so all these sadistic police officers will have to find some other way to spend their time other than hiding behind the billboard. So, if you want to punish these irritating people, just keep voting for the crowd who wants to stop all forms of energy development in the world, which will naturally cause more of these cool gas shortages, causing prices to go up even higher, forcing more and more of us to walk instead of drive. And since most of us can't walk fast enough to get to work on time let alone get pulled over, eventually, we will lose our jobs and become so poor that we will have nothing else to do except don a loin-cloth and frolic in the rainforest...as long as we don't need to eat.

HABIT No. 26

Placing a copy of your bounced check next to the cash register so everyone knows about it.

What you can do about it: Some would advise you to treat a shady, poorly-run business like this with contempt and simply stop patronizing the place, especially if they will no longer take your checks, forcing you to pay with cash, which you obviously don't have. However, we have what might be a better idea: Figure out some way to get a check from that business (if you have to you can send your 7-year-old daughter over there selling cookie dough to raise money) then, photo copy their check, stamp "insufficient funds" over it, and put it on YOUR wall or next to YOUR cash register. Then, send them a picture of it and see how they like it.

HABIT No. 59

Expecting me to solve my own problems.

This can be a major irritation. I mean, why should I be forced to figure out how to pay for my own retirement, or to pay for my own health insurance, college, computer, car, house, or how to get off drugs, or find a job? This is not right. People who demand that I do this are highly irritating and should be stopped. However, I also believe that I should not be expected to figure out how to make them stop. This is giving me a headache.

HABIT No. 60	Running you over with a car.

This probably requires no explanation. Since you will probably be dead, there is probably also nothing you can do about it. Sorry.

HABIT No. 61	The habit of interrupting your messaging, tweeting, or blogging and wanting to have a

good old-fashioned conversation with you.

There is possibly nothing more irritating than having your important electronic entertainment interrupted by human beings who have no idea what is truly important in life. It seems like the same people have the habit of doing this interrupting over and over again:

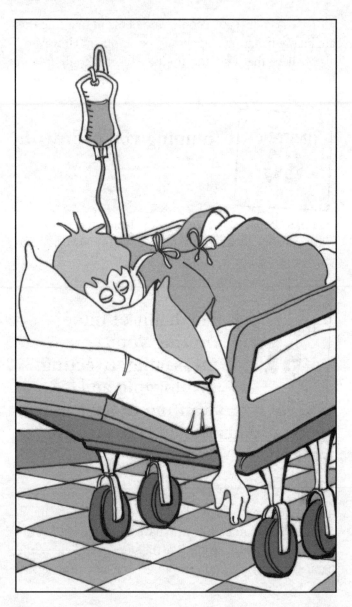

your spouse, parents, kids, friends, family—all those people who should know better, and who should have plenty of other opportunities to bother you, other than RIGHT NOW when you're in the middle of messaging. I mean, there you are in your very own basement, minding your own business, shopping on E-Bay for a pet pit bull or piranha, texting 7 of your old classmates, tweeting about the latest war in the middle east and the Lakers game, when out of nowhere you get blind-sided by one of the people who is very close to you and should know better who, because he or she is so familiar, just assumes he or she can waltz into your life at the drop of a hat and ask you a question pretty much any time he or she wants to. For example, your wife sidles up and asks you if you remember the conversation from the last time she interrupted you, and if you had made any decisions about how you were going to pay the medical bills for your daughter's treatment for lime disease and the spread of your wife's liver cancer. Of course you have no opinion on those subjects because you have not had time to consider them since the auction is wrapping up and you need to get one more bid in, AND your War Games buddy is going to sign off in one minute and for 10 hours you will lose the opportunity to confirm your strategy.

I'm sure that everyone has had this experience. It may be helpful to note here that this frustrating habit is fundamentally exactly the same as the old fashioned frustrating experience of trying to watch an important episode of Jeopardy or Gilligan's Island and having your kid, spouse, neighbor, or whomever, barge into your front room and want to talk to you about something as trivial as the impending death of a dear friend or your child's emotional problems.

So here's what you can do about it: If you really want to irritate the people who are bothering you in this way, have an extra blackberry sitting there, and hand it to them. Tell them they can use it to get on line and communicate with you like everyone else does, or else they can just go away. After all, who do they think they are?

Moral justification: Why should he or she be allowed to speak directly to you without going through some electronic device? What makes him or her think he or she is so special?

HABIT No. 110

Designing the engine in your car or truck so that it is impossible to change the oil in it without scraping your knuckles.

What you can do about it: Cussing the engine compartment, and those small-handed, pencil pushing, black tie wearing mechanical engineers who designed it, seems to help. Try this for a while, and if you don't get relief, try to get someone you don't like to change your oil for you.

Filming you in your hospital gown while you are on anesthetic and your backside is exposed and then posting the pictures on the Internet.

What you can do about it: Photoshop his or her head onto the torso in place of yours, thus showing what appears to be his backside sticking out, and then broadcast it all over the internet.

Bragging about how cheap the cell phone, (vacation, car, or other product) he just bought is, after you just bought a similar item and paid much more for it than he claims he did.

What you can do about it: Lie-claim to have just bought something he just bought and claim to have paid a tiny fraction of what the item is actually worth.

Moral justification: It's possible that he is also lying about how much he paid for the item he's bragging about. It's virtually impossible to prove one way or the other. Turn about is fair play.

Playing rap, kazoo, elevator, or some other uber-obnoxious type of music in the cubical or room next to yours.

What you can do about it: Find some even uber-er-obnoxious type of music and turn it up even louder than the stuff he's making you listen to.

Moral justification: Into every life a little rain must fall.

Using exactly the same weight-loss program as you are using, and losing weight much faster than you do.

What you can do about it: Eat extremely unhealthy, calorie-filled, but yummy stuff such as potato chips, peanut clusters, Moose Trax ice cream, or double-bacon cheeseburgers and fries in front of him and offer him some. Even if he or she happens to have the inner strength to resist your offers, you will end up with ill health, which will cause everyone's health insurance premiums to rise to cover the cost, thereby costing him or her more money. Touché!

Moral justification: Tests of character like the one you are putting him or her through will make him or her much stronger in the long run.

 Being better looking than you are.

What you can do about it: 1. Send her Krispy Kreme donuts twice a day. 2. Give her a jar of mosquitoes, wasps, or bacteria that causes splotches to form on her face. She may still be better looking, but at least she will go crazy itching. 3. Fill her shampoo bottle with Gorilla Glue. This will last for quite a few weeks.

Moral justification: No one should be allowed to be both smart AND good looking and you can't do anything about the smart part.

 Having a booger or some other indistinguishable fleck of material on his lip, cheek, forehead or nose.

What you can do about it: very discreetly point it out to as many other people as you can.

HABIT No.

125

Noticing that you have a booger on your lip and not saying anything about it... at least, not to you.

Actually, I can go you one better than this. I will share with you a highly personal, intimate, and sensitive true-life experience.

A number of years ago, I had a series of business appointments scheduled. While driving to my first appointment, I was irritated by my chapped lips. So I stopped at a C-store to get some chap stick. I bought the Chap Stick and applied it right there in front of the cashier, got back into my car and drove to my next appointment. Late in the afternoon I finished my series of important business meetings, and headed home. On my way home, I stopped at a convenience store and went inside to buy a soft drink. On my way in, I looked up into the rounded mirror (the one which lets the cashier see behind the aisles) and saw my reflection. I noticed that I had some bright red stuff smeared around my mouth ala Bozo The Clown. I reached into my pocket and pulled out my Chap Stick, which, upon inspection, turned out not to be Chap Stick at all, but was in fact cherry red lip-gloss. Unbeknown to me I had been providing entertainment to other sadistic people all day and no one had said a word about it to me.

"So, where does this leave us?" You ask. I have no

idea, but, having poured out my heart in confession of a terribly embarrassing experience, I am now way too emotionally drained to come up with any solutions to this problem or any moral justification. So you're on your own here.

| HABIT No. **127** | **Pointing out the flaws in your ideas and plans.** |

This habit really bothers me. Anyone can point out the flaws in somebody else's plans or ideas. It takes someone special to actually go out into the world and come up with original flawed ideas. Besides, if no one ever put flawed ideas and plans out there, we would wind up with grossly under-trained and unskilled critics, and cynics, since they would have no practice. Things are bad enough now, but can you imagine our world if it was filled with critics who didn't have any idea what they were complaining about? So, whenever someone points out the flaws in your ideas or plans we think you should do something about it.

What you can do about it: I think the best thing you can do to the people who find flaws in your ideas or plans is to work real hard to find the flaws in their characters and the characters of their relatives and friends. For example, let's say you are planning to start a business where you plan to become a veterinarian, who specializes only in skunk veterinary medicine. And some cowardly critic, who lacks vision and ambition, criticizes your business model on the basis of his concerns that the market for domestic skunk veterinarians is probably very small, possibly even too small to support one full-time skunk veterinarian in your market area. So, you could take on this know-it-all critic by doing what any good presidential debater would normally do in a situation such as this: launch vicious personal attacks against him. For example, you could say something like: "What kind of an idiot would assume there's no market for skunk veterinarians, especially when he personally dresses like Lady Gaga, cheats on his concubines, bounced a $50.00 check at Wal-Mart last month, and has a brother on drugs? People who swim in rancid cesspools shouldn't throw anvils."

HABIT No. 129 Driving poorly.

Here's an example: I was driving along the other day at about 10 MPH on the freeway talking on my cell phone. Six-feet of new snow had fallen overnight and it was still snowing heavily. The driving conditions were treacherous to say the least, with the road surfaces covered with hockey rink-quality ice and a thin layer of slush on top, which had accumulated since the last snowplow had passed a few years earlier. I had an important appointment to get to.

As we all know, the outside lane is reserved for less important vehicles and for those who had already experienced the thrill of spinning out of control for a split second or two into the barrow pit, off the side of the road; or even the consummate adrenalin rush of going into the opposing lane of oncoming traffic where the other drivers could test their skills at avoiding a head-on crash on an icy road. Once with an experience like this is usually enough.

On the other hand, the inside lane is reserved for those who had never had the thrill of these experiences before, or for those who had them, but for whom the head trauma had caused them to forget those experiences; And for drivers who are hard core adrenalin junkies who had been deprived of their rush for a few days and who get a thrill out of helping others to share their adrenalin rush with them; or for those who are simply boorish, self-centered idiots who are incapable of considering the safety of others. You never know which of these crazies is cruising in the inside lane way too fast for conditions. But for certain, these people have their lives filled with very important places to go, certainly important enough to risk your life.

So there I was working my way to my appointment in these wretched conditions, when one of the above-mentioned thrill seekers flew by in the inside lane. As luck would have it, Newton's laws of physics had not yet been suspended in our part of the world, and the snow on the road, when acted upon by the tires of this very heavy vehicle, was launched in the direction of my

vehicle. Other annoying laws of physics converged, sending the heavy, half-frozen slush onto my windshield completely covering it with an inch or so of frozen goo.

Unfortunately there are no wavelengths on the light spectrum capable of penetrating this brown-gray-white-thick substance, and my wipers were not equipped with plutonium to melt it quickly. Despite my total blindness to what was going on around me, miracle of miracles, I saw red. Were it not for my advanced age, I might have enjoyed the adrenalin rush, after all, I survived to write about it; however, I am at a stage in life where I no longer relish tempting fate, and so I would have preferred not to have had this thrill. I will give this six-year-old driver in an adult body the benefit of the doubt, since he hadn't bothered to ask me whether or not I wanted a thrill, and hence, had no way of knowing this, and since he hadn't bothered to ask me or the other drivers who he had slimed into blindness, I am including him or her in my list of 857 highly irritating people. It's the least I can do.

Another irritating hot shot who needs to be on the list. Since we are taking a look at irritating drivers, let's examine one more who deserves to be on the list. On another fine day, I found myself driving along on the highway amid fairly heavy traffic. The inside lane opened up, and since I understand that the speed limits are designed for vehicles like the Beverly Hillbillies' model T loaded with all their belongings and Granny on top in her rocking chair, and for my buddy, Dave whenever he takes an uncovered load of tree branches, grass clippings, and moose entrails to the dump in his 1974 Ford truck complete with 375,000 miles, all on the original tires, I speed. I know the highway patrolmen understand that my car is more recently inspected than these, and so are OK with me driving 15-20 miles per hour over the speed limit without needing a ticket.

Anyway, back to my second story: So, I was driving along only 20 Miles per hour over the speed limit, and I had just moved into the inside lane to get around the Clampets, who were going 25 MPH under, when in my rear-view mirror, on the horizon, I caught a glimpse of a blur. Thinking it must be an F-16 pilot flying low, a UFO or something, I dismissed it for a couple of nanoseconds. The next thing I knew this blur turns up 4-inches from my bumper acting perturbed, feverishly moving back and forth, trying desperately to find some way to get his smokin' hot rig onto two wheels so he can squeeze between my car and the Clampets.

Not being able to resist having a little fun and honestly wanting to cheer this tense guy up, I moved back and forth a little so he couldn't' get past, even on two wheels. Then I touched my brakes ever so lightly, just enough to make my brake lights come on and slow down just a little.

It was obvious that this stunt driver was having a bad day, because my attempts to get a smile out him went nowhere. So, eventually, I moved on past the Clampets and allowed him to fly past...literally...with clenched fists and giving me the old one-finger-salute, all because I was trying to brighten his day and lighten his load. (It didn't occur to me until later that he may have been hurrying because he needed to go to the bathroom.) So I am now content knowing that I have actually been one of the 859 irritating people, and that this guy deserved to have to contend with me, and that I am including him in my list of 859 irritating people not because of the hundreds of smoking vehicles he has chased off the road, or because of the mangled corpses he is responsible for, which are now lying at the side of the road, but because he has no sense of humor, which we find reprehensible in this grim, annoying, uptight world.

And, while we're speaking of having no sense of humor, let's also mention another one of our highly irritating people who deserves a spot near the top of the list:

One more highly irritating person who needs to be on the list: Beulah.

Now I don't mind if ill-advised-shallow-thinking hipsters create a thriving enterprise, the purpose of which is to fleece thousands of lonely animal lovers, praying on their tender hearts and sensitivity, because I am one and I am sure I have been fleeced a few times; however, I would like to point out that millions of HUMAN children starve, while wormy stray dogs and cats live out their lives cruising along in the canine or feline equivalent of a college dorm on full-ride scholarship.

I'm actually OK with that part. On the other hand, I struggle with some of these not-for-profit corporate executives' complete lack of a sense of humor, especially given the fact that these spoiled fraternity rats are getting stinking rich preying upon old and lonely folks' money and getting away with it, while thousand s of others, who have had to resort to schemes like roofing scams, selling drugs, or even to common burglary in order to fleece the aged and lonely, are languishing in jails around the country. And still they have no visible sense of humor. This is not fair.

What we can do about it: About all I can think of to do is encourage their senses of humor through pranking. In the unlikely event that a good prank or two doesn't improve their senses of humor, at least it will lighten the blood pressure of us pranksters. We just need to come up with an appropriate stray animal sanctuary prank. Maybe we could do a prank like when the Animal rights activists pull those clever pranks on dairy farmers, poultry farmers, and furriers.

HABIT No.

355

The habit of performing surgery

This is one of my pet peeves

and a terribly irritating habit. Everybody I know who has to deal with people who do this to them is absolutely miserable afterward. It doesn't matter if it is a hip replacement, back surgery, open heart, or whatever. Surgery is a rotten thing to do to someone. I think we should stop.

| HABIT No. **356** | **The habit of making mistakes in my checkbook and bank accounts.** |

Whenever there's an error, the banker is always right in the bank's favor, never mine. About twice a year, I wind up with a mess in my account that is so complicated it could probably have military secret code applications. Since neither me nor the bank have any idea how this happened, it's not fair that I should have to straighten out my own mess.

What we can do about it. I have absolutely no idea. Some people advocate that we all stop banking altogether. Pull all your money out of the bank and put into your child's piggy bank, your mattress, pickle jar, or just send it some worthy charity like me. This will eliminate this frustration altogether. Or you can lobby to get Congress to pass a banking regulation where we consumers get to have a minimum of half the mistakes resolved in our favor. 50-50 seems fair to me.

Moral justification: You are a free, sovereign individual who had the God-given right to choose whether or not to put your money in the bank or whether or not to give it to me.

HABIT No. **357**	**The habit of doing research to find out that all yummy-tasting food will kill you and then having the**

audacity to publish these findings.

What to do about it: I think they should set up a sliding scale of good foods. The better tasting the food, the more confidential the information about the unhealthiness of it. So if it were really yummy, it would be virtually impossible to find out that it will kill me. On the other hand, if the food is lousy, they can publish nutritional information all over the place.

HABIT No. **358**	**Bursting my bubble as to why my ideas won't work.**

What to do about it: This is pretty easy. All you have to do is find a flaw in the idea put forth by the person who found a flaw in yours. Let me give you an example. Let's say you have come up with the terrific idea of plugging up the hole in your septic tank using egg cartons and duct tape, which you just broke into pieces with the bucket of your backhoe trying to move the concrete piece next to it. And while you're working on this, your wife comes out and tells you she doesn't think the duct tape will hold because of the amount of moisture in your septic tank and that egg cartons probably won't hold out any of the smell, and so you should make another lid from concrete or use steel or something. You would come back with an argument like, "Have you ever seen a piece of steel that has covered a septic tank? Do you know what it looks like after 75 or 80 years? Covering this tank with steel or concrete would look awful, smell bad, and won't work. And another piece of concrete will just break again like this one did."

While she is pondering a response, you should have time to finish the project using egg cartons and move on to something else.

Moral justification: You are the guy, which makes you omniscient and omnipotent.

People who use my money to further causes and purposes that are bad, and which I don't support.

For example, when I taught in the public schools in Washington State union dues were taken out of my check each pay period. I was happy to support my colleagues' efforts through collective bargaining to negotiate a fair compensation package, bearing in mind that we were feeding from the public trough and in effect shaking down our neighbors and friends for our compensation, also bearing in mind that I got my summers off, and, depending upon which subject was taught and what age the students were who were being taught, many of my colleagues in public education finished up their work day at 2:30 in the afternoon while people in the private sector who were paying our salaries got off at 6:00 or later.

And of course, there are some jobs in the private sector that ruin a part of your life, for example, I love Chinese food, but if I worked every day in a Chinese restaurant, after a while I would probably learn to hate it, therefore taking away a very pleasurable and important part of my life. I'll bet the guys who do the stunts on motorcycles at the state fairs learn to hate the fairs, and when they retire or die in a ball of flames, they will never want to ever go back to a state fair, thus taking a huge part of their lives, and so teaching's not such a bad gig, I didn't think. Except I'll bet there are some people in education who end up not having any kids of their own because the sight of kids makes them sick to their stomachs, and who end up working in a Chinese restaurant thus destroying two important parts of their lives. But that's not the point. In fact, may of you are probably wondering, "What is his point?" So you will have to work with me here while I figure it out.

Additionally, I didn't agree with many of the political causes being espoused by my union bosses, such as keeping the union bosses' families in employment on six-figure incomes for life, or supporting people protesting on Wall Street who had no idea how the non drug-stupified world really works.

What you can do about it: Actually, I don't know, but I can tell everyone what NOT to do, because I did it. That is, I began working to opt out of my union dues, at least the part that supported union bosses families and political causes and had nothing to do with collective bargaining, and so I began the process of having my union dues reduced from $60.00 per month to $20.00. After a year or so of hard work and follow up and thousands of dollars in legal fees, I succeeded in getting my dues reduced and felt smug and proud. Unfortunately, this was not a precedent that someone more influential than I wanted established, and so about a year later, I get a letter explaining that I couldn't do what I had done and that they were going to hit my check for all the money that had not been withheld, which should have been. And they did. So I'm thinking that probably wasn't the proper approach for me to have used. So you may not want to try that.

HABIT No. **568**

The habit of yanking on your shorts to make you turkey trot.

Actually, this hasn't happened to me for many years, but I remember that when I was a kid I hated this.

What to do about it: I don't know.

HABIT No.

569

Having girls scream and run the other way when you try to ask them out.

What to do about it: Choose girls with laryngitis, I guess.

HABIT No.

570

The habit of telling you that what you are eating is unhealthy.

(This habit is very similar to another habit listed above. You will have to watch for the subtle differences, which make this a separate habit.) In this world there exists a biological truth that the tastier the food the less healthy it is for you to eat it. The opposite is also true: the less healthy the food, the tastier it is. Since everybody with an IQ in excess of 3 is well aware of this fact, it devolves upon us to do whatever we choose with that information. We don't need someone else to remind us. Whenever I eat yummy food, you can be sure that I feel overwhelming guilt knowing what it's doing to my health.

So whenever someone reminds you that what you love to eat is killing you, here's what you can do about it: You can disguise the yummy food. Wrap your donut in spinach leaves, sanctimoniously carry your transparent water bottle filled with pureed broccoli and sprouts into work with your bacon double cheeseburger hidden discreetly inside your briefcase, or keep your fudge brownies tucked inside your sock where you can sneak a bite whenever no one's watching.

HABIT No.

571

Giving out those irritating little ketchup packets, which, can only be opened with your teeth.

I'm sure that the ketchup or other dressing inside the packet is as clean and sanitary as it can be, but the guy who handled those packets while filling up the bin, dropped them into the goats' corral earlier in the day after running the plumbers' snake down the sewer pipe to clean out his septic system, delivered a litter of baby pigs, and pinched the pus out of the inflamed Staph infection in his nose, all after going to the bathroom without washing his hands.

What you can do about it: In order to get the ketchup or whatever, out of the obnoxious little packet, set it onto the floor and stomp on it while holding the French fry, which you want covered in ketchup, six-inches from the place you're hoping the ketchup will come out. If you are wrong about where it comes out, just grab another packet and try again.

Moral justification: If it takes you a few hundred tries to hit your French fry, that's OK. The amount of actual ketchup or other condiment in the packet is so teensy that the cost of all the ketchup in a few hundred thousand packets is much less than the cost of treating the disease you are likely to get from the germs on the outside of the packet or from the repair of your teeth.

What we can do about it (2): Bring our own ketchup, A-1 Sauce, or ranch dressing.

HABIT No. 572 — Being smarter, or more talented than your kid.

What you can do about it: I don't know, but whatever it is, don't do something you're going to get arrested for. This will put you on the same infamous list as a whole slew of out of control parents and your kid will probably think you are an old nerd anyway.

HABIT No. 573 — People who try to collect the money you owe them.

I don't know about you, but what really torques me off is people who heap the guilt on me and accuse me of being a deadbeat just because I haven't paid my bills to them. What an affront to my honor and integrity! I mean, if you had the money, you would pay your bills, right? Assuming, of course that you want to, and that this particular debt is more important than, say a new I-pod.

So who do they think they are anyway? This is a tough economy. It's a jungle out there and sometimes people get behind on their commitments. So, if I bought materials from you and I happen to be a few months late paying, just chill out. I've obviously had a surprise expense of some kind come up: medical bills, car breakdown, and a critically important vacation. Whatever the problem is, you can be sure it's way more important than your dumb bill. Knowing all this, you must know that when you call to bug me it is the height of offensiveness. Have some class! I'll probably move you right up to the top of my list as soon as I need something from you.

What, then, can be done about it? Of course, the simple way to shut people like this up would be to pay them what you owe them. But then that would probably just encourage them, and you would be likely to get more of their obnoxious behavior. This would most likely cause them to keep bugging the other people who owe them money, too. Since you probably don't want to make things that much worse, maybe you should try another tactic like paying someone else you owe money to the exact same money you COULD have paid them, and do it right in front of them with pomp and ceremony and great drama so they see what they are missing. This assumes that you have the money to pay them and you actually want to pay them. Otherwise, just get a new cell phone number.

HABIT No. **778**	**Voting for the wrong candidates.**

This is a really annoying problem. Apparently, most of the people who do this also vote many, many times because some pretty goofy people manage to get themselves elected to some pretty important positions.

What you can do about it. What I always do about this is refuse to take any responsibility for the mess things are in, because your guy didn't get elected.

HABIT No. **779**	**Speeding up in his car when I try to pass him.**

I have actually written about this before in a previous book, so I will refer to that chapter for a description here. I will, however, point out that people who do this-and there are many of them-are super annoying and they will probably be responsible for my death, if some freakish mutated bacteria from a public restroom doesn't get me first.

HABIT No. 780

Being more successful or better than me.

Some people are such jerks. In virtually every field imaginable, business, sports, music, academics, there are people who are just way better at things than I am. And I hate it. Whenever you encounter someone in your field that is better than you, here's what you can do:

1. Share dysentery with them.

2. Get them watching or listening to the news and they will become so discouraged thinking that the world is coming to an end that they'll lay down and quit, in order to have more time to feel sorry for themselves.

3. Slip bedbugs into his or her bed. He or she may still whoop you, but at least he will itch like crazy while he's doing it.

HABIT No. 781

Disagreeing with my philosophies of life.

As I analyze life, I have created a continuum, which looks like this:

This continuum is also three-dimensional, not just left and right. I have concluded that my opinions are the standard against which all others should be measured because I happen to be the ONLY one who pretty much always manages to get things right. So, on my continuum, I place myself in the center. The day that we will have peace, prosperity, and happiness in this world is the day when somehow we bring everyone into complete harmony with me. Conversely, the further we deviate from my opinions, the worse things will get.

In recent days, nearly everyone deviates to some degree, hence, there is much pain and suffering in the world. On the one hand you have all those people who agree or who very nearly agree, and on the other hand you have those goofballs who are way out there in the ozone. There is obviously much work to do.

Take for example, sports officials. I see what I see on the court or the field. I am not blind; therefore one can logically assume that my call is always true or right...unless, of course, I wasn't paying attention because I am cleaning up the blob of mustard off my shirt, or if the people sitting next to me distract me by wanting my opinion on strategy, play-calling, defense, or even the call itself, or if the guy selling concessions got in front of me and blocked my view, or if I happened to have bad seats or a bad camera angle, or, or something in my eye, or in the rare occasion when I wasn't paying attention. Pretty much all the rest of the time, you can be sure that I would be the standard against which all good officiating calls should be measured. So we can reasonably put my call in the middle of the spectrum.

It is amazing to me that there are sometimes thousands of people who see the exact same call as me and yet, if the official sees it correctly, too, they become upset. I just figure that these are the people who are dishonest or who are neurotic and refuse to deal with reality. The more violently they disagree with my call, the further they are out there on the fringes of the spectrum; also, the farther they are out there on the spectrum the more they often yell and are violent and get all worked up. So we have a huge bunch of violence at athletic contests, and in the world at large. If everyone would just agree with me, and see things the way things truly are, we world have peace and harmony in the gym, on the field, and in the world.

This principle carries over to all parts of life. Being in the exact harmonial vortex of the continuum of life, which is true reality, when it comes to politics, social problems, personal relationships, or basketball officiating will bring us all peace and harmony in our world.

What we can do about it: Obviously, we should devote our lives to getting everyone to agree with me.

HABIT No. **782**

Sharing your rap, hip-hop, opinions, or kazoo music with other people who don't want to hear it.

What we can do about it: See above. We obviously need to work to get everyone to agree with me on the correct types of music and opinions to listen to.

| HABIT No. **783** | ## Bragging. |

Years ago, some air-headed goofball came up with the mantra: "It ain't bragging if you can do it."

Pardon me, but bragging is bragging even if you can do it. If you can do it, you don't need to brag about it. People will take notice and want you on their team...unless of course, you are an obnoxious, socially inept, braggart, in which case they will assume you CAN'T do it, or that you are narcissistic, spoiled, immature, and insecure, because they know that most people who CAN do it don't want to brag, unless they are socially inept goofballs, in which case, even if they CAN do it, nobody wants to have to listen to that.

| HABIT No. **784** | ## The habit of owning the dog who jumps up and sniffs you. |

What you can do about it: This is a hard one to figure out. Some pretty nice people are capable of allowing their pets to jump up

onto their guests and shed a pound of hair onto them without seeming to notice or care. Not in all cases, but at least in some, I know these are people who are oblivious to social etiquette, or who don't have success with actual human beings in their lives, and so most of their friends are dogs, and so they lavish affection onto their dogs and treat people poorly. And at the rare times when human beings come into their homes, these people and their dogs don't know how to act. The rest of the people who allow their pets to do this, seem to otherwise be kind of normal, I have no idea about them. You're on your own. I guess you could always drop YOUR dog, which also jumps up and sniffs everybody, off at his or her house, giving him or her an example of what it feels like when this happens.

HABIT No.

787

The habit of failing to call the mutt off.

How to deal with him: In the case of the guy who doesn't get it, there is no known cure. Therefore, you can have a little fun with him. When his dog jumps on you, paint Sparky bright green, or squirt your stinky aunt's perfume onto his damp, little nose. Another fun way to get some enjoyment is to scoop his doo doo off your lawn and put it in the front seat of his owner's car with a note that says "Thanks, I'm trying to quit." Or "Thanks, but we use horse droppings in our garden."

HABIT No.
820

Being forced to hit a target on the move.

Whenever a person is shooting a gun, almost anyone can hit a bull's eye if he or she is allowed to take his or her time and rest the gun on top of a solid object known as a dead rest. Hitting a target while on the move or when distracted is another matter altogether. This is why you have to hand it to most guy-drivers. Almost anyone can drive along the highways of America and avoid accidents if all they have to do is drive by themselves without distractions. But it takes a real man to arrive alive at the appointed destination when, for the entire drive, he is getting last second, and often conflicting instructions shouted at him from the ladies in the car. That's why driving while under the influence of helpful women is on our list of 857 habits.

What you can do about it: Refuse to allow other helpful backseat drivers to travel with you when you are driving. You can also install a sound proof, bulletproof section of plexi-glass between the front and back seats and encourage the back seat drivers to ride in the back. If you are on a budget you can try turning down your hearing aid. Just be aware that if you choose this route you may be unable to hear important things like emergency vehicles and the sound of a van full of killer ninjas speeding up from behind.

| HABIT No. **821** | # The habit of scoring way higher than the class average on tests. |

This is truly annoying when everybody in the class gets below 32% on the Zoology 315 final exam. You got a respectable 30% and with the curve are expecting a completely acceptable A-minus for your final grade, when out of nowhere comes the word that some extreme nerd got 97%.

What you can do about it: For starters, I would certainly avoid taking classes like Zoology, Biology, and Physics, where you are likely to find a whole bunch of nerds, and concentrate on subjects like Recreational Management.

| HABIT No. **822** | # The habit of being so selfish as to grouse and complain in public when politicians want to use your money to |
buy other people's votes and otherwise spend your money in the way the politicians tend to do.

Apparently these wonderful altruistic purposes, which are clearly more important than making car payments or paying lame utility bills or saving for retirement, are keeping said politicians in power. The assumption is that if they don't take your money from you and use it properly, that you don't have enough character to do the right thing and give it to the group they want you to give it to, that you, personally have no idea exactly how much money you can spare for charity, and you lack the judgment to discern who is truly needy.

Coincidentally, your sanctimonious politician and his friends who are passing these judgments on you are either being paid by the government using these same dollars taken from you, and have conveniently passed laws exempting themselves from having to contribute to or even use the same programs you have to. Also, those people who they deem worthy to receive the money coincidentally keep voting them back in so, the money will keep coming.

What you can do about it: Ignore their complaining. These people are probably just selfish and immature.

| HABIT No.
823 | **Wearing cologne that makes people nauseous in the car you're car-pooling in.** |

What you can do about it: Retaliate and smear onions all over your briefcase and make it a point to step in some doggie doo on your way in.

HABIT No.

824

Calling to pretend he or she is a hot girl asking you for help on her homework, or work project.

This is a truly mean thing to do. You know what a rotten trick this is when someone does it to you, so you will only want to pull this prank on people you really don't like, or who have a real good sense of humor.

HABIT No.

825

Chaining a concrete barrel to your car bumper.

You were just going into the theatre for what you thought would be only10 minutes, but the movie you went to see turned out to be a 2-hour marathon.

HABIT No.

826

Watching you without your knowledge

Especially while you're doing things like picking your nose, tormenting the neighbor's irritating cat, or accidentally picking and tasting a sprig of grapes at the market.

HABIT No. 827

The habit of looking weird.

This is a tough one. Some people look weird because they look weird and there is nothing they can do about it. Some people look weird on purpose to get a rise out of other people like you. Some look weird because they are desperate for attention or because they want to be accepted by some weird group that is desperate for attention.

What you can do about it: Obviously, one method of dealing with weird people is: Don't look at them. Another way is to try to look even weirder than they do. One way of doing this is to wear a cow costume. Many places this would be considered really weird. This will not improve your chances of getting a good job.

HABIT No. 828

Driving five miles per hour below the speed limit.

This is cruel, especially to people who need to drive at ten or fifteen miles per hour OVER the speed limit to get to their important place on time.

What you can do about it: The tried and true method of breaking people of this habit is to camp out two inches behind their bumper and look angry. This will work great as long as he or she doesn't stop suddenly, AND if he or she isn't really big and really mean or armed with automatic, nuclear, or biological weapons.

| HABIT No. **829** | **Getting to an important, or secret place before I do.** |

People who do this are mighty annoying. Examples include: the times when I have hunted all over Rock Springs, Wyoming for a motel room late at night in July. I finally get sent to what I believe to be the very last motel that still has a vacancy sign on, and I make a beeline for it. I then open the door for and get to stand in line behind the guy who gets the last room.

And: I hear an amazing song by an artist I've never heard of before. So I root around and question everyone I run into about this song in order to find out who it is so I can share it with my friends, who are already familiar with it.

And: You can't wait to share a piece of juicy gossip, but they've already heard it by the time you get to the hair salon.

And: You have a great secret hunting spot down by the river. You arrive just as Ernie Schwartz emerges from the thicket carrying three Canadian geese, two mallard ducks, a rabbit, and a coyote.

What you can do about it. Beats me. Speed up, I guess. (See previous commentary on driving.)

HABIT No. **830**	**Bringing more than ten items into the express check out line at the store.**

What you can do about it: Obviously, you can move to another express line, unless the line wraps around the store three times like it does most Saturday nights and whenever you need to make a quick dash into the store. You can also take the good Sam route and offer to take some of his items and put them into your cart, and pay for them in order to keep him under the limit, or, you can take the bad Sam route and raise a ruckus and blow the whistle on this inconsiderate jerk and make a big scene, file a class action law suit or something. If you don't find any of these things to be satisfactory, have your two-year-old wipe his runny nose on this person's grocery bag out of contempt.

HABIT No. **831**	**Visiting with the teller at the drive-up window.**

What you can do about it: Use your bumper to push the offending car forward and into the street, complaining all the while that your car is out of control and won't stop.

HABIT No. 832

Young people who make a big deal about your advancing age.

One of the traumatic experiences of my life occurred while I was still a relatively young man, way too young to join AARP or legally receive senior citizens discounts, or possibly even be expected to have a bi-annual colonoscopy. And it happened as I was minding my own business totally undeserving of a traumatic experience.

At lunchtime I dashed into KFC to get an original recipe two-piece chicken order with two-sides. The place was rocking with children of tender age, sensitive women, and all kinds of people who also did nothing to deserve to find themselves in the middle of an explosive controversy, or to hear things that were crude, offensive, or untoward. Nevertheless, on this fateful day, with dozens of innocent people standing around within earshot, it came my turn to order. The young lady behind the counter appeared to be in her late teens, but it's hard for someone my age to tell. (For all I know she could have been in her early teens or in her forties), but that's not the point. I'm sure if you had asked any of the other patrons, they would have verified that I looked as normal as a long line in front of drivers license office, as common as a seagull at the land fill, as un-exceptional

as a pimple on the forehead of a teenager. Again, I emphasize: I did nothing whatsoever to deserve this rough treatment I as about to get. So I placed my order.

And then all of a sudden, as if this had been a moment of destiny and fate planned in the eternities by the powers of heaven, the place grew quiet, as silent as a tomb, as peaceful as the chapel in church after an inappropriate joke is spoken over the pulpit, as still as a baseball stadium of a losing team. We're talking ear-splitting quiet of the unsettling kind. It seemed that every ear in the place was trained in my direction. Despite dozens of the aforementioned tender, innocent people, who were capable of giving a deposition, the girl taking my order asked me:

"Would you like the senior citizens' discount?"

Caught completely off guard, I had no response. How could someone like me be prepared for such a question? To this day I have no idea if I said yes or no. I'm not completely certain if I even paid for my chicken. All I know is that with the words, "would you like the senior citizens' discount" ringing in my ears, the chicken was too bitter to eat. I realized later that this particular chicken had given its life for nothing. The chicken went to waste.

On the bright side, having been thus traumatized, when subsequent insults occurred, I was now prepared. That first brutal slam steeled me for other such slams and biting words. Over the years I have had many opportunities to respond to the question, "Would you like the senior citizens' discount." So, I guess in that way, having that gum-chomping teen say those words made me stronger and more prepared to deal with the tragedies and challenges of life.

What can we do about this habit? You can do whatever you want to. I'm planning to sue KFC.

| HABIT No. **833** | # Doing all kinds of things that make you nervous. |

When your children are young they make you nervous when they climb up on top of the back of the sofa and teeter back and forth, or when they run fast on a slick floor in their stocking feet, or when you turn your head for a minute and when you look at them again they have the legs of the pet gerbil sticking out of their little mouths. When they get a little older they make you nervous when they drive or when they leave with their friends for the evening, or when they tell you that you have nothing to worry about when you know perfectly well that you have all kinds of things to worry about. The people you elect to political office make you nervous whenever they are in session because you know that they are up to no good and it will cost you a bunch of money.

What you can do about it: Becoming nervous is an age-old coping mechanism for dealing with the stresses of being surrounded by idiots. Unfortunately, so are neurosis, psychosis, alcohol and drug abuse, the Jerry Springer Show, liberal politics, and animal torture. So that you don't get addicted by one of those, we thought it would be a good idea to give you some tips of how to deal with your nerves. In order to do this, we first need to give you a little understanding of how your nervous system works:

How your nervous system works. Your nervous system is made up of tiny units known as "nerve cells" or sometimes called, "Rodney Ganghaerfiel.d." Each of these is connected to all of the other similar nerve cells by electrical impulses called Bob. Think of these tiny messages as microscopic spit wads which one nerve loogies through a straw he saved from lunch, and which then splats onto the head of the next little nerve cell who picks it our of his ear (symbolically) straightens it out and reads the little note, then puts it into his straw and loogies it into the ear of the next little nerve cell and so on. Where we run into trouble is when one little nerve gets sick of being whacked in the head with a paper wad and retaliates, loogiing something other than the important little message back into the eye of the first one, and then another joins in and another until we have a giant neurological spit wad fight on our hands and someone gets his eye put out. This is what mental illness looks like metaphorically. So you see, we need to be careful here and not get too worked up about any of this stuff or bad things could happen. This would be the condition known as stress.

10 Excellent Methods For Relieving Stress
1. Beating your head on the concrete
2. Better yet, beating your head on a sack of cotton
3. Floating over a small waterfall on an air mattress
4. Putting your cell phone in the microwave
5. Putting your cell phone in the blender
6. Using your cell phone as a hockey puck
7. Listening to the sound of classical music
8. Listening to the sound of your car backing over your neighbor's teenaged son's boom box
9. Listening to the sound of running water-unless, of course, you are strapped to a table and the running water is dripping onto your forehead.
10. Escaping from the pressures of life by reading a side-splitting humorous book written by Ben Goode. (This has also proven to make you live longer and healthier, and become filthy rich.)

HABIT No. 834

Making me work

How to Avoid Working:
Using all the data made public on the internet, and in your on-line bank and cable company, and government data files, we have done extensive research on you, our readers. Yes, we know about all your purchases. We know what sites you have visited on line. We know your medical history.

We even know all the things that happened in Vegas and that stayed in Vegas, because although they're still in Vegas, Vegas is now on line.

After studying this research we have received an epiphany: The reason why you have been buying tons of lottery tickets is because you hate your job. What's great about this information is that now we know that if your judgment and math skills are really that bad we don't have to be all that smart to figure out a way to get you to give us some of your dough. So like all the crooks out there who are getting rich after mining your data, it's just a matter of time before we, the only HONEST hustlers out here, figure out a way to exploit your habits, vices, and weaknesses. Meanwhile, we need to garner your trust by giving you what we promised to give you a few minutes ago which is some ways to avoid working. So, here they are:

A Few Ways to Avoid Working

1. The easiest way is to have health issues. Maybe the best health issues you can have are mental issues, because the person evaluating your case most likely has some, too, and isn't likely to be very tough on you, and because mental issues are pretty tough to disprove. If you claim you're crazy, who's going to argue that. Look at you life!

2. Vote for the politicians who promise to give you the most goodies. Hey, they've got plenty of money and the stupid guy who's working like a dog and paying taxes to support all these programs is way to stupid to

come to my seminars or buy my book so we're definitely safe. And the politicians don't care. Most of them never worked an honest day in their life, so they wouldn't know the difference anyway. They think all the wealth and capital in the world came from previous politicians of their party. So you're probably safe there too.

3. Get a job where you get to work on line. Every computer guy I know who has a computer at his desk works for a total of about 15 seconds downloading something that makes it look like he's working, and then spends the rest of his day role-playing Darth Dragon. Whatever you do, don't get a job doing something like laying concrete, repairing diesels, or milking cows, because there just aren't very many easy ways to pretend you're working when you're not. You're pretty much open to anybody's criticism.

HABIT No.
835

Being Nuts

It really stinks to have to deal with nutty people. I would imagine it's even worse if you, yourself are nuts and are trying to get through life as a nut case.

How to tell if You are Sane or, How to be Sure You're Not Insane. Ask yourself the following questions. If you answer "yes" to just one of these things it may not, in and of itself, be a sure indicator you are insane. Don't get me wrong; it's not necessarily a good thing to honestly answer "yes", but if you score high on a whole bunch of them, you can probably figure you're nuts. Be scrupulously honest...unless, of course, you start noticing that you are answering, "yes" to a bunch of them. In this case, if it were me I would lie to myself in order to salvage my sanity and some self-respect.

1. Have I recently decided to run for public office?

2. When I pause from banging my head on the cement for a moment, do I lose my ability to think clearly?

3. Do I collect my drool in case I need it later? (This would not be an indicator of your insanity if you are saving the drool so that you can pretend to be insane later in order to get out of a tight spot or to avoid having to do work as described previously.)

4. Do I make my fashion statements with changes in the style and color of my straight jackets?

5. Do I have regular meaningful and intense conversations with my pets or with the voices in my head?

6. Do I regularly find myself peeling the paint off from my walls or car and eat it and do I offer to share it with my imaginary friend, Melvin?

7. Do I own a small publishing company or other small business?

8. If I do own a small business, do I expect it to be profitable in my lifetime?

9. Do I claim to understand what my wife is thinking?

10. Do I keep doing the same things in my life but expecting different results?

HABIT No.

836

Being a pushy, overbearing, obnoxious voice in my head.

The secret here is to be able to differentiate between the good voices and the bad ones. Here are a few tips I've learned over the years:

Are the Voices in My Head Good Voices or Bad Ones?

Voices are probably your friend if they tell you when your fly is open or when you have a booger on your lip.

They are not your friends if they tell you to obey Adolph Hitler, Jeffrey Dahmer, or Al Franken.

They are probably not your friends if they command you to obey your cat, hamster, or goat.

Voices are probably good who taste your food for you to make sure your ex-spouse didn't poison it...on the other hand, if they taste it until it's all gone, or encourage you to eat tofu, probably not.

Good voices will warn you when a dump truck is coming. Bad voices will lie about the dump truck and lure you into the street on promises of parade candy or so you can view the flattened carcass of your neighbor's irritating Chihuahua.

Good voices will settle you down, calm you when you are about to do something you will regret. Bad voices will remind you how satisfying it will be to dump a bucket of paint onto her and her friends from the mezzanine.

Good voices remind you that everybody will eventually find out if you lie about being at the library when you were breaking into the concert through a side door. Bad voices tell you that you smell fine.

Voices that tell you to take all your clothes off in the bank and run around screaming because they wouldn't loan you the money you wanted are likely not your friends.

Voices that tell you the government is your friend, and that there will be no strings attached if they give you goodies, are probably not your friend.

It's probably good to resist voices that make up songs about torturing the neighbor's cat. On the other hand, voices who tell you the guy you're dating, the one who all your family and friends hate, are a creep are probably OK.

I wouldn't trust voices who try to convince you that you can fly.

The ones who prompt you to say insulting and sarcastic things to your IRS agent, judge, drug supplier, or gang boss should probably be avoided.

I wouldn't trust the ones who prompt you to say insulting and sarcastic things to your wife either.

Stay away from the ones who would have you stockpiling weapons and ammunition for some "big event", but they won't tell you what it is.

I would definitely avoid the voices who try to convince you to sneak up behind your neighbor's Rotweiler and goose him.

Likewise, avoid the voices who would convince you to sneak up behind your Tai Kwan Do instructor and goose him.

I would stay away from the ones who try to convince you to climb over the big, iron fence so you can go talk to the president.

Incidentally, Here are a Few Things That You Can't Blame on The Voices in Your Head:

1. Your poor motor skills.
2. The habit you have of picking your nose.
3. Your kids' habits of picking their noses.
4. Your appendicitis.
5. The allergies you have to your roommate's cat.
6. Your lack of education.
7. Your inability to get a date.
8. Your poor memory.
9. World hunger.
10. Global Warming.
11. Nothing on TV is worth watching.
12. The foul smell in the room when you're alone.

One more Thought About the Voices in Your Head
There comes a time in everyone's life when they know that it's time for the voices to move out. Many voices are reluctant to go. Some simply refuse. This is when it is time to pull out all the stops and make life so miserable for the voices that they will move on gladly. Sometimes you just want to tease the voices to sort of lighten things up a bit. Whatever the reasons why you want to annoy the voices in your head, here are some proven ways to do it.

How to Annoy the Voices in Your Head
1. When they try to talk to you, hyperventilate until you pass out.
2. Respond to them after inhaling helium.
3. Mimic them and repeat everything they say.
4. Hum "La Bamba", or some other annoying tune, over and over again for years.
5. Choose a couple of words like aluminium or nucleulur and mispronounce them for the rest of your life…oh, and find reasons to use them regularly.
6. Sleep on top of a diesel generator.
7. Work on a really obnoxious cackling laugh and do it over and over again for things that are not funny.
8. Sleep next to a water buffalo.

HABIT No. 837
Interrupting me when I am whining.

I think it is really inconsiderate to interrupt someone when he or she is whining. All too frequently I just get started explaining about some important principle of life, which the whole world needs to understand, and just as I am building into a crescendo of eloquence, the person I am explaining things to interrupts me wanting to leave. This is very bad manners and highly irritating.

So, if you are ever listening to me explain something like "types of torture appropriate for politicians who spend my tax dollars inappropriately," or "what our generation would have done to the Mexican drug cartels", and "why we might have to come out of retirement in order to deal with all the problems in the world", be considerate and don't interrupt me. View this as a great learning opportunity. The rest of your life will probably still be there when I'm done explaining.

HABIT No. 838
Failing to know what I want.

This habit often leads to...

HABIT No.

839 Not doing what I want

...after I have dropped many subtle hints about what I want. This will likely force me to have to ratchet up the intensity of my "hints", possibly even forcing me to start resorting to...

HABIT No.

840 Yelling

...at you, which, if this fails, I may have to even try...

HABIT No.

841 Threatening to beat you up.

If you are so knot-headed that by this time you still have not picked up on my hints as to what I want you to do, about the only things left would be...

HABIT No.

842 Beating you up

or…

HABIT No.

843 Threatening suicide.

Wouldn't life just be a whole lot easier if you simply tried to concentrate a little harder and pick up my subtle hints in the first place and do what I want you to?

HABIT No.

844 Blogging

Yes, we are now blogging. Notice that we use the pronoun, "we". We do this because we want to acknowledge the valuable contributions of the voices in our head and keep them happy. So far throwing them a bone like this seems to minimize their tendencies toward subterfuge, and mean-spiritedness. Having resisted the urge to blog for many years, we have finally succumbed to the changing financial markets and the need to make some actual money in this rotten economy.

857 Habits of Highly Irritating People

Travel to exotic places where our books are displayed like Grand Canyon, Vegas, Yellowstone Park, and Battle Mountain, Nevada (town motto: Who are you and what do you want?) is down substantially from a few years ago, which has adversely affected our loyal readers' ability to get to our books. We are therefore bound and determined to bring bits of humor to our readers via the blog. We are doing this partly because we want to try to generate some money, but mainly because we want to reduce the time some of our loyal readers have on their hands with which they are free to do more devious and destructive things. We know our readers (don't we voices).

So we hope you will enjoy these bits of thought and odd perspectives. Our intent is to try to bring a guffaw or two into your otherwise strange and bizarre lives, not to just make people confused or angry as has sometimes been alleged. Therefore, if you enjoy these blogging bits, please feel free to share them with friends; if you don't enjoy them, feel free to keep it to yourself.

If our blogsite should some day disappear from the blogosphere, it is probably for one of the following reasons: 1. We got tired of blogging. 2. We ran out of ideas. 3. Nobody cared. 4. The technology changed again and now there is some new social media craze we have to try and figure out.

A brief note to you other technophobes out there, who will now be angry with me because you believe I have sold out going on line. I'm not the only author who has sold out. In fact, I should probably point out that some pretty famous, hard-core authors and artists have eventually sold out just like me. Take for example, J.R.R. Tolkein who sold the movie rights to his trilogy a few years ago from his casket in south central England, making for himself and family literally billions of dollars while sacrificing the integrity of his books only slightly to the editors, artists, and screenwriters inter-pretations of his work. Okay, I know some of you will insist that Tolkein, himself, had been dead for at least thirty seconds before his greedy, grasping heirs compro-mised his integrity when they sold the movie rights for billions, and that you might be OK with me selling out for billions, and that possibly even YOU would sell out if you thought you could make that kind of money, while Ben Goode is selling out for what amounts to chickens feed in the literary world. In fact, because he is such a dipstick around technology, it's entirely possible that Ben Goode will fizzle in his attempt to sell out on line, making it all the more pathetic…to which I would respond, "you're ugly and your mother dresses you funny."

| HABIT No. **854** | ## Having a life that stinks |

It's entirely possible that your life stinks. Since very often a person's quality of life is good or bad completely because of his or her percep-tion, we want to make you feel better if we can, and so we're going to try to give you a little different perspective.

A Different Perspective

How many times have you had an experience like having your college professor form your class into groups to do a project and announce that he's going to grade you not just on the quality of YOUR work, but based largely on the drivel contributed by the rest of your group which consists of:

1. Green-Hair-Boy, who still isn't sober enough to be sure whether this class is English 1010 or Ping Pong 350, who will turn in the same paper he has turned into every other class he's ever taken, namely the 150 pages his girl friend wrote on Jon Bon Jovi to keep him from being flunked out and having his dad cut off his expense account, and who hasn't been sober since his freshman year in high school.

2. Chatter Queen, who does everything she can to make it impossible for your group to ever get down to the actual work of doing your group project. If she had her way, you would spend the entire semester talking about doing your project, or preferably, talking about stuff that has absolutely nothing to do with your group project.

And 3. Phantom Man, who doesn't come to class, and has no idea what the project is even about, and whenever you get together to work on your group project, he forgets to come. The rest of you are stuck wrestling with the decision to just do his part of the project for him, or risk getting down to the deadline and having him flake out on you. Of course, he will get the same grade as everyone else.

You should begin to feel better when you finally figure out that YOU are the normal one and THEY are nuts. You are having a normal, healthy reaction to being assigned a group project like this, which is to think, "This doesn't seem right," to ponder, "what kind of teacher/professor would have a goofball assignment like this?" and to ask ones' self "Am I nuts?"

While it is possible that you are indeed nuts, a more likely possibility is that a high percentage of the people around you, including your college professor and the human sit-com skit known as "Your Group" are nuts. They have lost their collective grasps of reality and are existing in some parallel dimension, which could cause your healthy perception of reality to look odd by contrast, elevate your blood pressure and trigger the primordial fight or flight mechanism in your brain stem that causes you to want to kill something, skin it, and hang its remains on the barn.

We have written this book because we have recognized the need to make a whole bunch of money and because we have recognized that you need a book to make you feel better and this could be it; at least we hope so. So you will definitely want to read this book from cover to cover over and over and over until you start feeling better or until you start killing animals and hanging their carcasses on your barn. And then you will want to encourage your sane friends to buy it, too, and do the same thing. Then we will both have a fighting

chance of succeeding at our goal of feeling better. Me, because I will have my car payment covered, and you because you will be proactive in your quest to deal with these nut cases who are injected all over in your life.

Having the voices in your head continually annoy you or talk you into doing stupid things

There comes a time in everyone's life when they know that it's time for the voices to move out. Many voices are reluctant to go and drag their feet. Many refuse. This is when it is time to pull out all the stops and make life so miserable for the voices that they will move on gladly. Sometimes you just want to tease the voices to sort of lighten things up a bit. Whatever the reason, here are some proven ways to annoy the voices in your head.

How to Annoy the Voices in Your Head

1. When they try to talk to you, hyperventilate until you pass out.

2. Respond to them after inhaling helium.

3. Mimic them and repeat everything they say.

4. Hum "La Bamba", or some other annoying tune, over and over again for years.

5. Choose a couple of words like alunimun or nucleulur and mispronounce them for the rest of your

life...oh, and find reasons to use them more regularly than a normal person would in every day speech.

6. Sleep on top of a diesel generator.

7. Work on a really obnoxious cackling laugh and do it over and over again for things that are not funny.

8. Sleep next to a water buffalo.

9. Completely ignore them as though they don't even exist.

10. Blame them for everything that ever goes wrong in your life, even if they had nothing to do with it-even if they warned you not to do the thing that caused the problems.

11. Tell them the same jokes over and over and over and over.

12. Tell them the same lame stories over and over and over and over.

13. Make them tend your kids regularly.

14. Make them watch really lame TV shows.

15. Go on a major political crusade and spend a few weeks talking about nothing about politics.

HABIT No. 856

Being completely unable to shut up.

This is a very perplexing bad habit.People with this problem seem to have more than just a little irritating habit. Apparently, this can become a full-blown addiction. It is especially dangerous when it is combined with unusually great physical yakking skills, which, for some reason, it usually is. I mean, how many times have you been hurrying off somewhere, or trying to finish up an important project with an actual important deadline, when some blathering office person moseys by and starts to yak in your direction. Because you have been cornered by this person before and narrowly survived, you know you are in trouble. So you take preemptive action and try to interrupt him or her in order to courteously explain that you are in a hurry. This does not even slow him or her down. You frantically look for a small opening between this person and the wall, or for a crack in the door, which you can slip out of, but he or she has closed off your exits like a pack of African dingoes cornering a wounded gazelle. You are trapped.

Since you were raised with a few manners, you wait patiently, all the time developing a tactful way of begging off. You are watching and listening intently for one tiny split second when this person has to stop to inhale a little air, thinking that then you can speak up and politely excuse yourself. Remarkably, these people often have lungs like bagpipes, because they can go on for hours or even days and weeks without allowing even a split-second pause for you to squeeze in even one word.

Listen to me. When you encounter people like this you are in a dangerous place. You must realize that this is a life or death situation. You could die here. You are in deep trouble. Did I mention that you MUST realize the seriousness of the situation? You must marshal all your strength and courage and use tough love.

Here is what you must do. In order to save your life and project or appointment, you must come up with a diversion.

Here are a few diversions, which have saved the lives of a few people:

A Few Diversions Which Could Save Your Life

1. Drop onto the ground, grab your chest, begin choking and start to quiver and writhe in agony. Keep one eye opened, and the instant he or she looks around to see if help is around, jump up and run for cover. Do not stop running until you are in a different time zone. Pray that he or she is not a world-class marathon runner or triathlete.

2. Get a look of terror in your eyes, look up, and point into the sky screaming, "air raid! Air raid!" The instant he or she glances up, run to the nearest restroom or janitors closet, dart in, and bolt the door. Sneak out the back window or through an air duct if you must.

3. Use your powers of imagination and imagine the most disgusting thing you can, until you get sick and throw up. While he or she is flabbergasted by the mess on the floor you have a split-second opportunity to dart in the direction of the nearest group of people. With any luck, you may be able to lose him or her in the crowd.

4. If you have practiced as a ventriloquist, without moving your mouth, begin to carry on a separate conversation. Speak quietly at first, then louder and louder until you are talking louder than this person. If

you can, throw your voice so that it sounds like it is coming from a nearby rock or cubicle. Not used to being interrupted, this person will likely become agitated or irritated. You are watching for the moment when he or she becomes irritated and looks a dagger in the direction of the rock or cubicle from where your thrown voice is coming. The instant his or her eyes leave you, run as fast as you can. Hide in a refrigerator or oven if you have to.

I know these are some pretty lame escape ideas, but this is really a tough one. I hope these work for you. If they don't, and if you survive, after you recover, spend some time with a six or seven-year-old who you know and who you can observe. From this child you can learn how to mimic other people, or you may be able to learn some knock-knock jokes or something so at least you can get even and irritate this person afterward. Good luck.

HABIT No.

857

Being a politician

Of course by now you realize that most if not all people in extremely important positions of power are nuts and that their insanity will have a huge bearing on the quality of your life – and there is absolutely nothing you can do about it. But, because there are other intelligent people in the same boat, you can spend a good portion of your future commiserating and moaning with your intelligent friends and using this insane behavior as a backdrop for some entertaining sarcasm and wit.

A case in point: I once questioned my very own sanity when a vice presidential candidate used one breath to very sanctimoniously lecture his audience about how the very complex and weighty decision to take out a million-dollar mortgage on a 10-year old double-wide trailer is a personal choice and only registered voters are competent enough to make it. And then with the next breath, he told all the same voters that they're not competent to take a voucher and choose which school their children will attend. With his third breath, he ranted about the depth of doo-doo the social security trust funds are in since he and his colleagues have embezzled most of the money and used it to buy votes and to cover up other poor financial choices they've made over the years. The fourth breath was used to explain that his constituents are not competent to invest their own social security retirement funds into stocks because those assets might drop in value! How did these clowns got elected to important national offices? And then re-elected?

The only rational way I have figured they could keep getting elected is through massive voter fraud. Then I had that theory shaken to the foundation by the realization that they're not smart enough to pull that off. That made me start feeling better until I realized they were still in charge. I finally concluded that the only way a sane person could cope with all this confusing reality is to chalk it all up to the fact that, once again, we are completely surrounded by idiots.

Now, armed with all of that knowledge, you can go forward with confidence, hope and optimism, knowing that there is enough material out there in everyday life to keep you and your friends knee deep in sarcasm and humorous material until you die or go insane. Enjoy!

More Apricot Press Humor Books

"In a world where some people may not want any part of your attitude, the sharing skills taught in this book are a must have."

Paperback $7.95 U.S.

"Maybe you're just sick and tired of being wealthy and you're ready to try something else for a change, like poverty. Whatever your circumstances, we know this book is for you."

Paperback $7.95 U.S.

"Instructions for becoming the Geezer you have always dreamed of. Geezing is not as easy as it looks. It's definitely not for sissies."

Paperback $7.95 U.S.

"This book is for the few who are silently bearing the burden of a superior intelligence, or think they are anyway..."

Paperback $7.95 U.S.

"OK, so you're having a bad day, maybe a whole slew of them in rapid succession. You've tried whining, you've tried complaining and nobody cares."

Paperback $7.95 U.S.

"If we are to understand the urge in man to fish, we must dig down through the strata of dirt and rocks and compost deep into the earth, back to primitive man to find our clues..."

Paperback $7.95 U.S.

"People today are worried. We worry that the economy will go into the tank, causing us to get laid off from our job as quality control tester at the dental floss foundry..."

Paperback $7.95 U.S.

"If you have seen more than a few sunsets, you may be starting to suspect that life is not fair. This book provides more evidence."

Paperback $7.95 U.S.

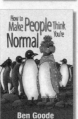

"If this book is in your hip pocket when a dog bites you, it could save your tattoo. It contains humor for people who are so smart, normal people don't understand them..."

Paperback $7.95 U.S.

"A must read for anyone trying to stay sane while driving on today's idiot infested roads."

Paperback $7.95 U.S.

Order Online! www.apricotpress.com

"What could possibly be more important than irritating the people who annoy you, thereby helping them pass through more trials so they will learn to become less irritating."

Paperback $7.95 U.S.

"Few things in life bring greater satisfaction than confusing idiots. This book is filled with great ways to do just that."

Paperback $7.95 U.S.

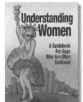

"Unless you are battling a case of terminal stupidity, you know that you need this book. Beginning with how to be sure someone is really a woman, this book explains it all."

Paperback $7.95 U.S.

"A book guaranteed to solve all your problems with guys...even the really dopey ones. Written by a certified guy!"

Paperback $7.95 U.S.

"A course designed to give remedial training to idiots so that they can function in society. Includes test to determine who is an idiot and things you should absolutely never do."

Paperback $7.95 U.S.

"This light-hearted parody on bathroom books belongs in every privy in America and the third world. Topics include: Pet Peeves, Bad Farming Ideas, and Fun with Vegetarians."

Paperback $7.95 U.S.

"In this classic you can learn how to maintain a good attitude after the world has hurled your decrepit body, or the body of someone you know, onto the trash heap of life."

Paperback $7.95 U.S.

"If the bags under your eyes are larger than your shoes, if your wife has more hair on her face than you do on your head... you need this book."

Paperback $7.95 U.S.

"This book explains to clueless people how to tell when someone is ornery, how to be miserable in the face of unprecedented prosperity, and other useful skills..."

Paperback $7.95 U.S.

Apricot Press Order Form

Book Title	Quantity	x	Cost / Book	=	Total

All Humor Books are $7.95 US.

Do not send Cash. Mail check or money order to:
**Apricot Press   P.O. Box 98
Nephi, Utah   84648**
Telephone 435-623-1929
Allow 3 weeks for delivery.

**Quantity discounts available.
Call us for more information.**
9 a.m. - 5 p.m. MST

Sub Total =

Shipping =   **$2.00**

Tax 8.5% =

Total Amount
Enclosed =

Shipping Address

Name:

Street:

City: State:

Zip Code:

Telephone:

Email: